Notes of Poetry: Learning Love

Luis R. Otero IV

Presentation by *BookLeaf Publishing*

Web: www.bookleafpub.com

E-mail: info@bookleafpub.com

ISBN: 9789357446242

First edition 2023

DEDICATION

I dedicate this collection to the emotional maturation of Jaxson and Gael. May you always remember the importance of understanding, sharing, and developing the emotional health of yourself and those around you. We are emotional and logical beings, neither aspect should be neglected.

ACKNOWLEDGEMENT

For the guides and examples offered by my family, my friends, the unbefriended, and the creator of my beliefs, I thank you.

PREFACE

In all situations experienced by humans, the common denominator is emotion. Please enjoy the challenge of finding your emotions in the journey of love throughout the storyline. It is expected for the reader to relate to different pieces with different levels of relation, in regards to their emotional palate. The constitution of their palate will dictate a personal interpretation in the moments of digestion. As time reshapes their constitution, it may also reshape their interpretation.

Please reflect and enjoy.

CONTENTS

Love: Exemplum

Love is equal in parts of fate and decision.

Those separate from decision, face the abuses
of desire.

Those separate from fate, indulge in the lost
feelings of neglect.

Notes:

Bound for Bandages

Two bandages wrapped the other,
Indulging survival's sport.
For neither were spun in patience,
Nor salvaged their wounds to sort.

With comfort in their lumps,
Torn hearts bled of clumps.
Both died to find truth,
For lies fashioned their youth.

Notes:

But, It's Good When It's Good

Eroded from the drafts of the day
I catch winds and wind up at your door.
Half of me hoped you wish I'd stay,
The other hoped I'd visit no more.

I know I've erred enough to give flight to your
hollowed-out wings.
I know our insecurities nest within each heart.
Yet, you burn in the alcohol soothing my stings.
Yet, we choose to drown in oceans pushing us apart.

It is a beautiful sight with a closed eye.
It finds us buoyant after we fuss.
Is it worth it to fight and then cry?
Does this mean we are fighting for us?

What is this, Love?

Notes:

Hardly Wasted

Even with the splashes you created, you understood
all would drift to the order of nature.

Nonetheless, a considerable amount of time is washed
on finding assurance.

Here, you finally find a bit and grab the flat rock you
stood on.

It's perfect.

With all of the effort left over, the rock is cast as a
preserver.

Assuming the previous heaves were anomalies, each
skip brings hope that the surface won't break up.

This time you count three. It might have been three
days, three weeks, three months, or three years.

A thought arises, holding the imagination in the
effort to be true,

But lying below, the water has already claimed the
rock.

Then it grips the corners of your eyes.

Frustration erupts as your mind seeks another rock,
promising grace upon time.

Notes:

The Talk

(Do you love me?)

                                         (Yeah, babe.)

(Do you actually love me?)

                                               (Yes.)

*This time answered with a growing smile of
confusion.*

(I don't love you anymore.)

In that moment,

*A teardrop seeped through the membrane of
the heart.*

*That blooded drop sunk into the well of that
chest,*

*Then eyes sprinted across the distance to
theirs,*

Half-expecting them to smile with humor.

*They were locked, but now radiated an aura
of relieved discomfort.*

                                   (So, now what?)

Pausing for a response.

(...)

Only closed, silent descent answered back.

Notes:

Voicemail

Hello, Voicemail.

This is my third time hearing from you today

Or technically the first time for today, two hours
past midnight.

Our first conversation was lighthearted

Almost a complete joke, entirely due to coincidence.

Our second conversation was long.

I felt foolish for wanting to hear from you again.

I told myself not to talk to you again.

Yet, here I am.

Our third conversation confirmed my regression

As the one-sided conversation rung in my ear,

As my breath held in fear,

As our conversation grew near.

Notes:

One Without One Will Never Be 2.

When I shower, I blanket myself with the warmed embrace of water as if it willingly rolls over my skin. Each drop with individual purpose to soothe, rinse, and quench the dryness of my opened chest; yet, showers never seem to remove the layers of muddled thought and recycled loneliness.

Out of my solitude, I find myself speaking to the sky.

My exhausted eyes inhale dry hope from the air of the approaching rain cycle. I watch as the clouds begin to form and then quickly prepare myself for a soulful downpour.

I run and place my buckets to collect falling pieces; I run and perform a rain dance to bait the storm from shying away; I run and open the shading nets that protect my crop from the overbearing rays of light;

And yet, it sprinkles.

Yet again, I am forced to dump half-filled buckets on dry crops. Yet again, my dance is shortened to find the returning beams of sun on my heartland. Yet again my eyes return from red to exhausted.

I question myself as I wait for the next perfect storm…

"Why don't I move?"

Notes:

The Moon

27

Love composed the world

That realized extinction.

Now cast as a moon,

It shifted in motion.

Revolving the Sun,

It still spun to orbit,

A new one was formed,

But still the moon floated.

Notes:

The Deep

Looking down, the fog drifted into focus.

As it condensed, a swim was forced for air.

A shiver of indecisiveness spread as a freezing
current brushed over.

In multiple directions, ladders breach into what is
audible,

But there are too many directions to focus on which
is right.

Frozen solid waves fall like dominos from above

And the surface loosens as it slips overhead.

There's more ease in ignoring all and saturating,

Suspended from progress, but suspended from chaos.

The drain pulls from below

And welcomes submission to the subtle movement,

Sinking forward, and carrying on with numbed
motion.

Notes:

30

When Noticed,

Loneliness arrived in these moments
unnoticed.

Pain finds the peeled heart from the
chest.
Ache in the skin begs a return to be
pressed.

Collapse to the ground, for reason
is hopeless.
Awake through the night, when
thoughts find their protest.

Stuck in the mind, a voice was left
broken.
Silence was found more than comfort
was spoken.

Loneliness thrived and forced upon
notice.

Notes:

32

Perfectly Televised

I stared at the TV.

It sat there, still and silent.

The chaos of colors combined in the emptiness of my eye, after I clicked the remote.

Then, I clicked again to study the silence of the hidden figure.

My eyes locked as I realized the reflection in the black of the screen.

Mysterious was the still, silent, and empty emotion that gazed between.

Notes:

34

Broken Windows

35

Bleeding tears expended,

For the soul broke

And the windows separating the world from it

Succumbed to swelling.

Notes:

Time Traveler

Half-consciously, Time stumbled until it tripped forward.

Thoughts escaped from sealed pockets during the unbalance.

The somersaults seemed to increase as more spilled out,

Until a distraction cut into the path of concentration.

Irrevocably lost, Time and the Traveler lie on the ground and steadied.

What felt like a moment delivered a receipt in aging,

Spent in the future, but of changing currency in the past.

Notes:

How Close Are You

As my eyes shut,

I began to forget the reflections of light and
darkness that governed me.

Soon forgetting to absorb the waves of force
clashing about me.

The air seemed to retreat to a tasteless waft of
acceptance.

My bones vibrated until my skin felt mute.

The cleverness of my tongue grew dumb over
sensations of numbness.

With clarity, the most profound thought seeps into
reality…

"I am Here."

Notes:

To Mature in Exposure

My heart, from hand to fate,

Falls with grace and a splash of pain over the edge.

As I was submerged, I forgot of air

And instead lived in the depths of your eyes:

A search for immortality in the imagination of your heart

A home not bound to brick and mortar nor to rigor and mortis,

A hiatus in loneliness from rounds of hide and seek.

My skin, from scars through games,

Grows with tolerance and a spark of flames within the chills.

As I was enlightened, I forgot of clouds

And instead lived in the depths of your eyes:

A traveler resurfaced from the desires of stories,

A happiness in which healing was more necessary,

A growth that was gained in self-appreciation.

As I fell apart, the shadows of my hidden pieces melted in the warmth of exposure.

Notes:

42

Through the Seasons

Piano petals fall,

Notes of nature spring.

Winter will melt us all,

Summer will ice the sting.

What we seek is to match,

But what is subtle is beauty.

Unable to grab, yet attainable.

Notes:

Mind, My Peace

I think I finally found it,

A place where the prevailing force is focus.

Here, I choose which waves coast along or crash
against the sand.

Ripples in the ocean balance with direction from my
hand.

Here, the weight of the air can avoid the judgment of
gravity.

Obstacles float according to the precedence of my
ascendency.

Here, I was once suspended to rest within poisoned
embryonic fluid.

Awards of salvation led me from the blind ingestion
to emerge lucid.

A place where prevailing is my realm to rule,

I conjure my reality.

This is worth protecting.

Notes:

Preparing for New

Then,

I kissed you again.

This time I felt the residue I left on your lips,

A slim film of saliva.

Too many before and many more kisses to offer,

Yet we still lie motionless.

Then, I found a path worth whittling down for.

There, I cut my identity from you and I.

Here, I fit to unlock my treasure.

Now, I have become the key for growth.

Now,

Kisses are fresh beside each minute.

Time is of better taste this second,

A glaze sweeter than sugar.

Expired suspense and now more patience to
offer.

Time has walked me into happiness.

Notes:

48

[Unlock]

As the key and lock combined,

What was once poised to defend against the world

And what was once aggressive to unlock it, fell to calm.

The combination formed for what became home.

It was the condition of each that became the cure for the other.

The lock was unrefined and blocky,

For fear of how the world would take from it.

The key was thinned and cut away from,

For fear of how the world would not accept it.

Yet now,

The lock found a reason to share its treasure

And the key, a reason to turn from the world.

Both eased the pain of anxiety,

To leave room for love.

Notes:

Closer than Hugs

I embraced our love when we hugged.
I could feel their heart flow to my mind;
My heart suckle upon theirs;

Their skin through fabrics of shirts,
Porous from the pain in their experiences,
But kindled from the kindness of their exposure;

The flames of their hatred rested in my grasp,
The living hell of life's emotions
With the tenacity to still oppose failure
And the humanity to fault by our reason;

The habit of their laughter engraved to memory,
The audacity to find humor
Amongst the constant destruction of hope or plans
And the vagueness of rebirthed opportunities.

I love this soul,
For I am a part of more than its vessel.
For we are whole,
Even when our bodies no longer nestle.

Notes:

Love: Denotation

Love /ləv/ n.

1)

2) The captured understanding of a given creator in which the camera is human expression and the photographer is self reasoning.

3) Trust in one brought by the ability to harness hope in desire and denial in death.

Notes:

9 789357 446242